EDGE
BOOKS ™

LIBRARY OF WEIRD

THE WORLD'S
WACKIEST
HISTORY

by Christopher Forest

Raintree is an imprint of Capstone Global Library Limited, a company incorporated in England and Wales having its registered office at 7 Pilgrim Street, London, EC4V 6LB – Registered company number: 6695582

www.raintree.co.uk
myorders@raintree.co.uk

ISBN 978 1 4062 9211 4
18 17 16 15
10 9 8 7 6 5 4 3 2 1

British Library Cataloguing in Publication Data
A full catalogue record for this book is available from the British Library.

Editorial Credits
Aaron Sautter, editor; Kyle Grenz, designer; Charmaine Whitman and Katy LaVigne, production designers; Pam Mitsakos, media researcher; Kathy McColley, production specialist

Photo Credits
Alamy: Niday Picture Library, 5; Corbis: Bettmann, 7, 23, World History Archive, 27; Getty: DeAgostini, 13, Popperfoto/Paul Popper, 21, Photodisc, 29 (bottom); iStockphoto: duncan1890, 11; Landov: Ivy Close Images, 15, UIG, 19; Library of Congress, Prints and Photographs Division, 9; NARA, 8; Newscom: CMSP Education, 25, sfgp/Album, 20; Shutterstock: Aerostato, 17 (top), Jay Boivin, cover, bonchan, 22, Derek Hatfield, 12, Anton Prado PHOTO, 26, Aptyp_koK, 16, Igor Sh, 28, stockcreations, 29 (top), Taratorki, 17 (bottom), worac_sp, back cover; Science Source: ANT Photo Library, 24; Wikimedia, Thomas Quine, 10

Design Elements
Shutterstock: AridOcean, KID_A (throughout)

Printed and bound in China.

CONTENTS

WEIRD AND WACKY HISTORY

Have you heard how crisps were invented? Do you know the real reason why pirates wore eye patches? And did you know that many important medical discoveries were the result of lucky accidents?

History books are full of information about important people and events. People often know the details of major wars or great leaders by heart. But history is full of many little-known facts that you won't learn about at school. Strange customs, crazy **coincidences** and uncanny tales often don't make it into history textbooks.

coincidence *something that happens accidentally at the same time as something else*

For example, you may know that Abraham Lincoln was a President of the United States. But here's something you may not know. As a young man, Lincoln was a champion wrestler! In about 300 matches, only one man was ever able to defeat him. Lincoln even holds an honorary position in the US National Wrestling Hall of Fame!

ABRAHAM LINCOLN

Facts such as these and many others are all part of hidden history. These stories can sometimes startle people or make them cringe. But they almost always capture people's imaginations. Read on to find out just how weird and wacky history can be!

CHAPTER 1
UNCANNY COINCIDENCES

Many stories tell of strangers who happen to have a connection to each other. There are also tales of people who happen to be somewhere at the best or worst possible times. History is full of these stories.

"MR TORNADO"

In 1948 Theodore Fujita saw the damage caused by a rare tornado in Japan. This experience sparked a desire to learn about these destructive storms. In 1953 Fujita moved to the University of Chicago, USA, to study tornadoes and learn how they work. After years of study, Fujita came to be known as "Mr Tornado". He developed a scale that measures the strength and intensity of tornadoes. A version of the Fujita Scale is still used by scientists today. Amazingly, Fujita did most of his work having never actually seen a tornado! He didn't personally see any tornadoes until 1982, near the end of his life's work.

TRUTH IS STRANGER THAN FICTION!

In 1898 Morgan Robertson wrote a book called *Futility*. It told the tale of a large ship that was thought to be unsinkable. But during its first voyage the ship struck an iceberg and sank. More than 2,900 passengers died. Fourteen years later, the real ship RMS *Titanic* struck an iceberg and sank in the North Atlantic Ocean. More than 1,500 people died in the disaster. Coincidentally, the ship in Robertson's book was called *The Titan*!

QUITE A SURVIVOR

Violet Jessop was quite a survivor. In 1911 Jessop was serving as a **stewardess** on the ship RMS *Olympic*. She was on board when the ship crashed into the HMS *Hawke* on 20 September that year. Jessop later served as a stewardess on the RMS *Titanic*, which hit an iceberg and sank on 15 April 1912. She survived that sinking and later became a stewardess for the British Red Cross during World War I (1914–1918). On 21 November 1916, Jessop survived again when the HMHS *Britannic* sunk after striking a mine!

stewardess *woman who serves passengers on a ship or aeroplane*

TITANIC SINKING

GEORGE WASHINGTON ... THE BRITISH OFFICER?

George Washington served as a colonel in the British army during the French and Indian War (1754–1763). He hoped to one day become a high-ranking officer, but he was never promoted. However, Washington was a born leader. He eventually became the leader of the Continental Army during the American Revolutionary War (1775–1783), as well as becoming the first US President.

LUCKY FOG

On the evening of 27 August 1776, George Washington found it hard to leave New York. During the Battle of Long Island, the British army had nearly surrounded Washington's soldiers. The British chose to wait until the following morning to attack. However, during the night a heavy fog rolled in to the region. Washington and his soldiers were able to escape unseen through the thick fog.

HOW PUZZLING!

During World War II (1939–1945), Leonard Dawes made crossword puzzles for *The Daily Telegraph* newspaper. But in May 1944 the British and US armies were concerned about some of his puzzles. Several of Dawes' puzzles had unique answers, such as Utah, Omaha and Overlord. These names happened to be top-secret code words used as part of the Allies' plan to liberate Europe on 6 June. However, after talking to him, military leaders soon realized that Dawes was just a skilled crossword puzzle maker.

FREEING THE SLAVES

The American Civil War (1861–1865) was fought partly over **slavery** and its importance in the South of the country. Although he fought for the South, General Robert E. Lee was never a strong supporter of slavery. He had inherited his slaves and chose to free them in 1862. Lee wasn't the only Civil War leader to own slaves. Union commanding general Ulysses S. Grant once owned a slave too, whom he freed in 1859.

ROBERT E. LEE

slavery *owning other people; slaves are forced to work without pay*

CHAPTER 2
CURIOUS CUSTOMS

Throughout history people from different cultures have followed many traditions. These customs once formed part of everyday life, but many of them seem very strange to us today. Let's take a look at some of history's most unusual traditions.

BURIED WITH THE SERVANTS

People in ancient China believed an emperor's servants could still be useful in the **afterlife**. They were buried along with the emperor so that they could continue serving him. A similar practice was used in ancient Egypt. Servants were sometimes put to death and buried with a **pharaoh**.

ASPIRIN, PLEASE!

For 7,000 years some doctors cured headaches with a drill called a trepan. Doctors used the device to drill a hole into a patient's skull. This process was believed to help relieve headaches, release evil spirits and treat the brain. Trepanning was used in ancient and **medieval** Europe, the Incan Empire, ancient Africa and Asia. The practice may have helped some people. But historians believe many patients died from having holes drilled into their heads.

SHAKE ON IT

Handshakes once meant much more than just a friendly greeting. People in ancient and medieval times used handshakes as a sign of peace. Shaking hands allowed people to show each other that they had no weapons and meant no harm.

STRANGE MEDICINE

In ancient China doctors were paid to keep people healthy, rather than healing them after they became ill. In fact, if a patient became ill, the doctor had to pay a fee to the patient! For doctors with important patients, such as the emperor, healthcare was a matter of life and death. If the emperor was unwell, the doctor could be executed!

afterlife *life that some people believe begins when a person dies*

pharaoh *king of ancient Egypt*

medieval *relating to the Middle Ages (c. AD 1100 to AD 1450)*

MAKE A WISH

Have you ever made a wish while breaking a wishbone? The ancient Etruscan people of Italy began this ancient custom about 2,400 years ago. They believed that chickens, geese and other birds were magical and could help predict the future. After eating chicken for dinner, they first allowed the bird's collarbone to dry in the sun. Two people then rubbed the bone to make a wish before competing to break it. People believed that whoever won the larger piece would have his or her wish granted.

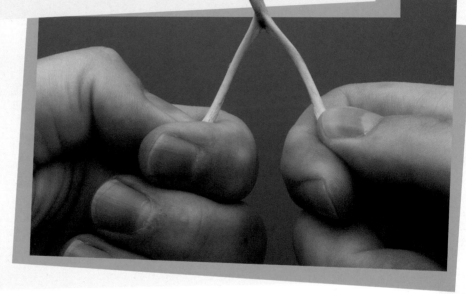

PATCHES FOR PIRATES

You may think pirates wore eye patches to protect injured or missing eyes. This might have been the case for some pirates. However, some historians think pirates wore eye patches to help them fight better in the dark. When going from bright sunlight into a dark room, it can take up to 25 minutes for a person's eyes to adjust. Eye patches could have helped pirates avoid this issue. When boarding a ship, a pirate could just move the eye patch from one eye to the other. The pirate's previously covered eye would already be adjusted to the dark, allowing him to see well in the dim light below a ship's deck. This gave pirates a great advantage when raiding ships!

TALK ABOUT A HEADER

In ancient Greece and Rome, people played a version of football that used human skulls for balls! Sometimes games were played across entire villages. The first team to kick the skull into the centre of the opposing village won. Nobody knows exactly what the prize was for winning these bizarre games.

CONE-SHAPED HEADS

If you had lived in ancient Peru, you might have had a cone-shaped head! Some wealthy Incan families tightly wrapped cloth straps around their babies' heads. The straps changed the shape of the babies' heads as they grew. Having a cone-shaped head was possibly a sign of wealth and high rank for the child and its family.

CHAPTER 3
ALL ABOUT THE TIMING

Sometimes major historical events take place because of unusual timing. In other cases, certain people happen to be in the right place at just the right time. If the timing had been different, then the following bizarre events might not have happened at all.

THE LAST SOLDIER

In 1972 hunters on the island of Guam got the surprise of a lifetime. In the jungle they found something remarkable – a Japanese soldier from World War II! Shoichi Yokoi had been serving on Guam during the war. But when Japan **evacuated** the island in 1944, Yokoi was one of several soldiers left behind. When he was discovered nearly 30 years later, Yokoi was the last survivor. He had survived by making clothes out of tree bark and eating rats, toads and eels.

evacuate *move away from a dangerous place, to find safety*

14

LANDING IN THE WRONG SPOT

The Pilgrims who travelled to America in 1620 settled in Plymouth, Massachusetts. But did you know they were actually heading for the Hudson River Valley in New York? At that time this area was actually part of the Virginia colony. It had plenty of farmland that the Pilgrims hoped to settle on. However, a late start to their journey and severe storms slowed down their progress. When they arrived in North America, they were further north than they had intended. Winter was about to begin, so the Pilgrims chose to settle in Plymouth, Massachusetts, instead.

PILGRIMS GREET AMERICAN INDIANS IN PLYMOUTH, MASSACHUSETTS

COLUMBUS' FIRST SALES PITCH

Before sailing for the New World in 1492, Christopher Columbus needed to find someone to pay for the trip. Columbus made his first "sales pitch" in 1484 to King John II of Portugal. He tried to convince the King that his journey would help make Portugal rich. But other experienced sailors told the King that the voyage would be too dangerous and expensive. The King turned Columbus down, which forced him to seek funding from Spain instead.

POWER OF THE MOON

In February 1504 Christopher Columbus and his crew were stranded in Jamaica. The people there soon grew tired of giving the Spanish explorers food and shelter and planned to stop helping them. Columbus decided to use an upcoming **lunar eclipse** to trick the people into continuing to help. He told them that the Moon would disappear if they stopped helping the sailors. When the eclipse occurred, it was very frightening. The people agreed to keep bringing food and supplies to help Columbus and his men.

lunar eclipse *astronomical event in which Earth's shadow passes over the Moon*

THE ACCIDENTAL CRISP

The first crisps were created by accident by an angry chef! In 1853 a customer at Moon's Lake House in Saratoga Springs, New York, USA, complained that his chips were too thick. When chef George Crum heard this, he became irritated and decided to take the customer's idea to the extreme. He cut some potatoes into thin slices and fried them until extra crispy. But to Crum's surprise, the customer loved the new potato "crisps"! The popularity of crisps soared and they soon became the salty snacks we recognize today.

USEFUL WAFFLES

In the USA in 1904 Arnold Fornachou was selling ice cream at the St. Louis World's Fair. Before long, he ran out of paper dishes to serve the ice cream to his customers. Luckily Ernest Hamwi was selling waffles in the next booth. Hamwi rolled up his waffles and shared them with Fornachou to serve his ice cream. The "ice cream cones" were a huge hit – and people have been eating them ever since!

CHAPTER 4
WACKY TALES OF DISCOVERY

Many useful scientific discoveries have been made throughout history. These discoveries are usually made by experimenting and following a plan. But sometimes amazing discoveries are the result of lucky accidents. Read on to learn a few amazing stories of scientific discovery.

A LUCKY HOLIDAY

In August 1928, scientist Alexander Fleming took a holiday from his research work on bacteria. Little did he know that his time off would end up changing medicine forever! When Fleming returned from his holiday, he decided to clean and reorganize his lab. As he was cleaning, he noticed that some mould had killed the bacteria in one of his samples. After further study, Fleming found that the mould could be used to make **antibiotic** medicine called penicillin, which is still used today.

antibiotic *drug that kills bacteria and is used to cure infections and disease*

FIRST VACCINE

When he was a young man, British doctor Edward Jenner spoke with a dairymaid as she milked a cow. She mentioned that people who got cowpox rarely got the dangerous disease smallpox. The dairymaid's words gave Jenner an idea. In 1796 he took samples of cowpox and gave them to an eight-year-old boy. The boy became mildly sick with cowpox, but was otherwise OK. Jenner later exposed the boy to smallpox, but the boy never got the deadly disease. Jenner's tests turned out to be the world's very first **vaccine**.

vaccine *medicine that helps to prevent a disease*

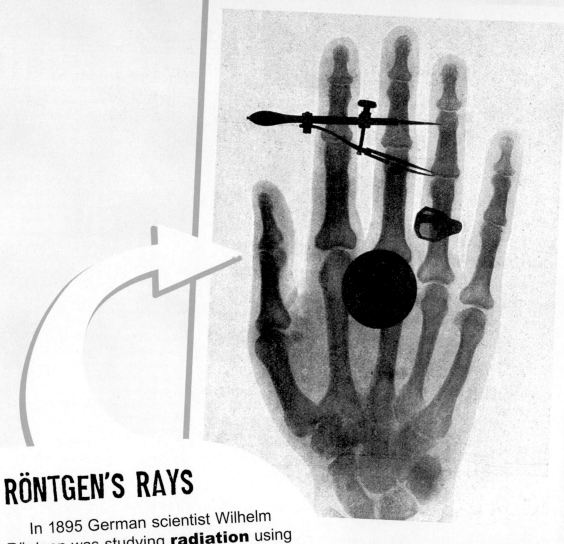

RÖNTGEN'S RAYS

In 1895 German scientist Wilhelm Röntgen was studying **radiation** using **cathode ray** tubes. During one of his experiments, he covered a tube with some black cardboard. At that point he noticed that a chemically-coated screen was glowing across the room. Röntgen realized that some kind of energy was passing through the cardboard to make the screen glow. He called this new energy "X-rays" and did more experiments. He found that X-rays could pass through many solid objects to form amazing pictures. Röntgen's discovery eventually led to the first X-ray machine.

radiation *tiny particles sent out from radioactive material*

cathode ray *beam of electrons*

FIRST PHONE

Alexander Graham Bell is known for inventing the telephone in 1876. However, Bell didn't originally intend to create the telephone. He was searching for a way to help deaf people communicate using a new type of **telegraph** machine. But Bell's experiments led him to create the "electrical speech machine", or telephone, as we know it today.

telegraph *machine that uses electric signals to send messages over long distances*

FIREWORKS!

Chinese scientists first invented gunpowder in the 800s. However, they didn't originally plan to make explosives. They were trying to invent medicine to help people live longer. But when they mixed together sulphur and other chemicals, the mixture easily caught fire and burned very fast. Soon the new substance was being used in weapons as well as exploding rockets that lit up the night sky.

RUBBER GUM

In 1870 Thomas Adams was testing sap from a tree found in Mexico and South America. He hoped the sap, called *chicle*, could be used like rubber. It failed. However, he knew the sap could be chewed for a sweet treat. He gave it a try and then got an idea. Adams used it to create the first flavoured chewing gum. Black Jack chewing gum was soon sold all over the world. In 1899 a new sugar-coated version was created and named after the sap used to make it. Chiclets gum is still popular in the United States today.

QUICK COOKING

The next time you heat something up in the microwave, be sure to thank Percy Spencer. During World War II, Spencer was working for the Raytheon Company, which made radar equipment for navy ships. While standing in front of an active **magnetron**, Spencer noticed the chocolate bar in his pocket began to melt. He realized that microwaves must have heated the chocolate enough to melt it. Spencer's accidental discovery eventually led him to create the first microwave oven.

magnetron *electronic device used for creating extremely short radio waves*

CHAPTER 5

THE TRUTH BEHIND THE STORY

Some historical tales are told so often that facts are sometimes forgotten or get changed as the stories are repeated over many years. Let's find out the truth behind some famous stories.

NOT-SO-NASTY VIKINGS

Most people think the Vikings were all fierce warriors who attacked and plundered villages. Viking raiders often attacked towns and villages, but most of the Viking people were simple landowners and farmers. They lived peacefully, grew oats and barley and raised animals.

WORKING FOR PEANUTS

George Washington Carver was an American scientist who became famous for finding about 300 different uses for peanuts. Many people believe that Carver also invented peanut butter. But it is one peanut invention he didn't come up with. People have actually eaten simple peanut pastes for nearly 3,000 years. Marcellus Edson was the first person to patent modern peanut butter in 1884. He added sugar to peanut paste and called it "peanut-candy."

RIGHT SIDE OF THE ROAD

French Emperor Napoleon Bonaparte was left-handed. He liked to keep his sword arm between himself and any would-be attackers. So while on his horse, he preferred riding to the right. Napoleon ordered that all the people he ruled over should ride on the right-hand side of the road. European **immigrants** later brought this custom to North America. This is why people there and in many other places drive on the right-hand side of the road.

immigrant *person who moves from one country to live in another*

PYRAMID BUILDERS

Many people think slaves were used to build the pyramids in Egypt. But most historians say these huge monuments for the pharaohs were actually built by farmers. The River Nile flooded every year. As a result of this, the farmers couldn't tend their crops during that time. Instead, they worked for the government and helped to build the pyramids.

HALLEY'S NAMESAKE

Many people believe that British astronomer Sir Edmund Halley was the first person to see Halley's comet. But the first records of the comet were actually made around 240 BC. Halley simply studied comet reports from 1531, 1607 and 1682. He believed the reports were all about the same comet and believed that it would return in 1758. Halley died in 1742. But in 1758 the comet returned, just as he had predicted. The comet was then named in his honour.

FIRST TO SAIL THE WORLD

Ferdinand Magellan is often thought to be the first person to sail around the world. He left Spain with five ships in 1519 and sailed across the Atlantic and Pacific Oceans. However, Magellan was killed in 1521 during a battle with islanders in the Philippines. Only one of his ships finished the voyage in 1522. Magellan's remaining crew of 18 men were actually the first to sail all the way around the world.

KIDNAPPED!

St Patrick is the patron saint of Ireland. But did you know that he actually grew up in Britain? He lived there until Irish raiders attacked his family home. They kidnapped Patrick and took him back to Ireland. He was then sold as a slave and made to work as a shepherd. Patrick eventually escaped. But he later returned to Ireland as a Christian bishop.

CHAPTER 6

STRANGE, BUT TRUE

We've seen stories of strange coincidences, unusual timing and accidental discoveries. You may find the following stories hard to believe, but they're all true!

WHERE'S THE TIN OPENER?

The idea of putting food in tins was developed in France by Nicolas Appert in 1795. He discovered a way to preserve food and store it for a long time in glass jars. Appert's process made sure the jars were sealed without air. He called his process Appertizing. Soon other food manufacturers began using tin cans to preserve food in the same way. Unfortunately, tin openers weren't invented until 1858 by Ezra Warner. Before they came along, people had to open tins with hammers and chisels!

THE REAL DRACULA

When most people think about Count Dracula, they think about the fictional bloodsucking vampire. But did you know that Dracula was named after a dangerous and cruel ruler? Vlad Dracul was born in Transylvania in 1431. From 1456 to 1476 he ruled over the area of Wallachia in southern Romania. Dracul was a violent ruler who would do anything to stay in power. He ordered the deaths of nearly 80,000 people. Thousands of those people were **impaled** on stakes and left as a warning to others.

impale *thrust a sharpened stake through a person's body*

THE YEAR WITHOUT A SUMMER

In 1815 Indonesia's Mount Tambora exploded in one of history's largest recorded volcanic eruptions. The volcano launched so much smoke and ash into the air that it affected weather around the world. In 1816 temperatures across Europe and North America were very cold. It was so chilly that year that people started calling it "The Year Without a Summer". Some parts of the eastern United States even had snow in June!

THE WAR FOR AN EAR

In 1731 British captain Robert Jenkins claimed that a Spanish officer had cut off his ear. Meanwhile, the Spanish claimed that Jenkins had been attacking their ships in the Atlantic Ocean. Over the next several years, tensions built between both Spain and England. Jenkins later presented his detached ear to Parliament in 1738. The hostility between Spain and England eventually led to a war that lasted from 1739 to 1743. The conflict later became known as the War of Jenkins' Ear!

THE NIGHT NIAGARA STOPPED

As the time approached midnight on 29 March 1848, Niagara Falls became quiet – too quiet. The next day very little water flowed over the falls. What happened? Large ice dams had formed upriver, blocking off the flow of water. People even walked and rode horses where the water usually flowed. But by 31 March the temperature had warmed up and the winds shifted. Water was soon roaring over the falls again as normal.

BIG FAMILY!

The first wife of Feodor Vassilyev holds the record for having the most children. According to records of the time, from 1725 to 1765 this Russian mother gave birth to an unbelievable 69 babies! These included 16 pairs of twins, seven sets of triplets and four sets of quadruplets. And Feodor Vassilyev later had a second wife who gave birth to another 18 children!

INVENTING THE SANDWICH

In the 1700s Englishman John Montagu loved playing card games. He loved it so much that he didn't like to stop to eat. So he came up with a clever solution. By placing meat between two slices of bread, he could eat and play cards at the same time. Other people followed Montagu's lead. His handy edible invention soon caught on and became very popular. It was even named after Montagu's title – the "Earl of Sandwich."

WILD AND WACKY HISTORY

History is full of well-known facts and dates. But it's also full of fascinating hidden stories. These stories show that history contains many strange events. See what other bizarre stories you can find. There's a whole world of wacky history out there waiting to be discovered!

GLOSSARY

afterlife life that some people believe begins when a person dies

antibiotic drug that kills bacteria and is used to cure infections and disease

cathode ray beam of electrons

coincidence something that happens accidentally at the same time as something else

evacuate move away from a dangerous place, to safety

immigrant person who moves from one country to live in another

impale thrust a sharpened stake through a person's body

lunar eclipse astronomical event in which Earth's shadow passes over the Moon

magnetron electronic device used for creating extremely short radio waves

medieval relating to the Middle Ages (c. AD 1100 to AD 1450)

pharaoh king of ancient Egypt

radiation tiny particles sent out from radioactive material

slavery owning other people; slaves are forced to work without pay

stewardess woman who serves passengers on a ship or aeroplane

telegraph machine that uses electric signals to send messages over long distances

vaccine medicine that helps to prevent a disease

READ MORE

Did the Romans Eat Crisps? And other questions from History (Questions You Never Thought to Ask), Paul Mason (Raintree, 2013)

Life in Medieval Britain (A Child's History of Britain), Anita Ganeri (Raintree, 2014)

What did the Vikings do for me? (Linking the Past and the Present), Elizabeth Raum (Raintree, 2011)

WEBSITES

www.bbc.co.uk/history/forkids/
Learn more about famous events, people, discoveries and inventions from world history.

www.bbc.co.uk/schools/primaryhistory/famouspeople/
Find out more about Edward Jenner, Christopher Colombus and many more famous figures from history.

www.britishmuseum.org/explore/young_explorers1.aspx
Follow the links to find fascinating facts from throughout history.

INDEX